Apple Trees

Helen Huus
Professor of Education
University of Missouri–Kansas City

Robert J. Whitehead
Professor of Education
Sacramento State College

Program Director
Henry A. Bamman
Professor of Education
Sacramento State College

Field Educational Publications, Incorporated
A Subsidiary of Field Enterprises, Incorporated
San Francisco   Addison, Ill.   Berkeley Heights, N.J.   Atlanta   Dallas

Apple Trees

Field Literature Program

Standard Book Number 514–01201–3

Acknowledgments

The order of acknowledgments follows the sequence of selections in the Table of Contents.

Grateful acknowledgment is made to the following sources for permission to reprint copyrighted material:

Illustrations from ''Hey Diddle Diddle'' by Randolph Caldecott, used by permission of Frederick Warne & Co., Inc.

''Firefly,'' from *Under the Tree* by Elizabeth Madox Roberts. Copyright 1922 by B. W. Huebsch, Inc., renewed 1950 by Ivor S. Roberts. Reprinted by permission of The Viking Press, Inc.

''One Is Good but Two Are Better,'' abridged and reprinted by permission of the publisher, The Vanguard Press, from *One Is Good but Two Are Better* by Louis Slobodkin. Illustrations by the author. Copyright, 1956, by Louis Slobodkin.

''Tommy,'' from *Bronzeville Boys and Girls* by Gwendolyn Brooks. Copyright © 1956 by Gwendolyn Brooks Blakely. Reprinted with permission of Harper & Row, Publishers.

''The Little Red Hen and the Grain of Wheat,'' reprinted by permission of G. P. Putnam's Sons from *Chimney Corner Stories* by Veronica S. Hutchinson. Copyright 1925 by Minton, Balch & Co.

Illustration of ''Jack and Jill,'' from *Mother Goose* by Kate Greenaway. By permission of the publisher, Frederick Warne & Co., Inc.

Illustration of ''Humpty Dumpty,'' from *The Real Mother Goose*, illustrated by Blanche Fisher Wright. Copyright 1916, 1944 by Rand McNally & Company.

''Hoppity,'' from the book *When We Were Very Young* by A. A. Milne, illustrated by Ernest H. Shepard. Copyright, 1924, by E. P. Dutton & Co., Inc. Renewal, 1952, by A. A. Milne. Reprinted by permission of the publishers.

A Tree Is Nice by Janice May Udry, pictures by Marc Simont. Text copyright © 1956 by Janice Udry. Pictures copyright © 1956 by Marc Simont. Reprinted with permission of Harper & Row, Publishers.

''Clouds,'' reprinted by permission of G. P. Putnam's Sons from *All Together* by Dorothy Aldis. Copyright 1925, 1926, 1927, 1928, 1934, 1939, 1952 by Dorothy Aldis.

''Spring Rain,'' from the book *Around and About* by Marchette Chute. Copyright ©, 1957 by E. P. Dutton & Co., Inc., and reprinted by permission of the publishers.

''One Was Johnny,'' from *The Nutshell Library* by Maurice Sendak. Copyright © 1962 by Maurice Sendak. Reprinted with permission of Harper & Row, Publishers.

Illustrators

Dave Broad: ''Who Likes the Rain?''

Ray Der: ''Clouds,'' ''Spring Rain''

Ed Tabor: ''The Little Red Hen and the Grain of Wheat''

Earl Thollander: ''Tommy''

Wendy Wheeler: ''Firefly,'' ''The Little Elfman,'' ''Star Light, Star Bright''

Contents

Hey Diddle Diddle

Hey, diddle, diddle,
The Cat and the Fiddle,

The Cow jumped over the Moon.

The little Dog laughed
to see such fun,

And the Dish ran away

with the Spoon.

Sharing Time

1. Why did the little dog laugh?

2. Where do you think the dish
   and the spoon went?

3. What part do you think
   is the funniest?

4. What does fiddle music
   make you want to do?

Who Likes the Rain?

Clara Doty Bates

"I," said the duck, "I call it fun,
For I have my little red rubbers on;
They make a cunning three-toed track
In the soft, cool mud. Quack! Quack! Quack!"

Firefly

Elizabeth Madox Roberts

A little light is going by,
Is going up to see the sky,
A little light with wings.

I never could have thought of it,
To have a little bug all lit
And made to go on wings.

15

One Is Good but Two Are Better

Louis Slobodkin

One is good,
But two are better,

You need two people
For a letter.

One pulling a wagon
Is not enough,
You need two
When the road is rough.

18

One can swing
Alone in the sun,
But you need two
To have more fun.

One in a boat,

Playing down at the shore

Can't go very far

With only one oar,

But if there are two,
Two oars and two friends,
You can row
'Round the world
Before the day ends.

One with a ball
Needs one with a bat;
Baseball is better
Played like that.

One can run,

Or one can lag,

But you need two

For playing tag.

One may hide,
Or one may peek,
But you need two
For hide-and-seek.

Yes, one is good,
But when there are more,
Say two or three
Or more than four,

You all can sing,
And you all can play,
And you all can have
A wonderful day.

Sharing Time

1. What can *two* children do?
   Draw pictures to show.

2. What are some of the
   sound-alike words?

3. What is the story
   trying to tell you?

Tommy

Gwendolyn Brooks

I put a seed into the ground
And said, "I'll watch it grow."
I watered it and cared for it
As well as I could know.

One day I walked in my back yard,
And oh, what did I see!
My seed had popped itself right out,
Without consulting me.

The Little Red Hen
and the Grain of Wheat

Retold by Veronica S. Hutchinson

One day the Little Red Hen
was scratching in the farmyard
when she found a grain of wheat.

"Who will plant the wheat?"
said she.

"Not I," said the duck.

"Not I," said the cat.

"Not I," said the dog.

"Very well then,"
said the Little Red Hen,
"I will."

So she planted the grain
of wheat.

After some time the wheat
grew tall and ripe.

"Who will cut the wheat?"
asked the Little Red Hen.

"Not I," said the duck.

"Not I," said the cat.

"Not I," said the dog.

"Very well then, I will,"
said the Little Red Hen.

So she cut the wheat.

"Now," she said,
"who will thresh the wheat?"

34

"Not I," said the duck.

"Not I," said the cat.

"Not I," said the dog.

"Very well then, I will,"
said the Little Red Hen.

So she threshed the wheat.

When the wheat
was threshed, she said,
"Who will take the wheat
to the mill
to have it ground into flour?"

"Not I," said the duck.

"Not I," said the cat.

"Not I," said the dog.

"Very well then, I will,"
said the Little Red Hen.

So she took the wheat
to the mill.

When the wheat was ground
into flour, she said,
"Who will make this flour
into bread?"

"Not I," said the duck.

"Not I," said the cat.

"Not I," said the dog.

"Very well then, I will,"
said the Little Red Hen,
and she baked
a lovely loaf of bread.

Then she said,
"Who will eat the bread?"

"Oh! I will," said the duck

"Oh! I will," said the cat.

"Oh! I will," said the dog.

"Oh, no, you won't!"
said the Little Red Hen.
"I will."

And she called her chicks
and shared the bread with them.

44

Sharing Time

1. What did the Little Red Hen do
   to get the bread?

2. Why didn't the Little Red Hen
   give any bread
   to the duck, cat, or dog?

3. How do you know the Little Red
   Hen was a good mother?

Jack and Jill

Jack and Jill
Went up the hill,
To fetch a pail of water;
Jack fell down
And broke his crown,
And Jill came tumbling after.

Humpty Dumpty

Humpty Dumpty sat on a wall,
Humpty Dumpty had a great fall;
All the King's horses and all the King's men
Couldn't put Humpty Dumpty together again.

The Little Elfman

John Kendrick Bangs

I met a little Elfman once,
  Down where the lilies blow.
I asked him why he was so small,
  And why he didn't grow.

He slightly frowned, and with his eye
  He looked me through and through—
"I'm just as big for me," said he,
  "As you are big for you!"

Hoppity

A. A. Milne

Christopher Robin goes
Hoppity, hoppity,
Hoppity, hoppity, hop.
Whenever I tell him
Politely to stop it, he
Says he can't possibly stop.

If he stopped hopping, he couldn't
    go anywhere,
Poor little Christopher
Couldn't go anywhere . . .
That's why he *always* goes
Hoppity, hoppity,
Hoppity,
Hoppity,
Hop.

A Tree Is Nice

Janice May Udry

Trees are very nice.
They fill up the sky.
They go beside the rivers
and down the valleys.
They live up on the hills.
Trees make the woods.

They make everything
beautiful.
    Even if you have
just one tree,
it is nice too.

A tree is nice
because it has leaves.
The leaves whisper
in the breeze
all summer long.

In the fall, the leaves
come down and we play in them.

We walk in the leaves
and roll in the leaves.

We build playhouses
out of the leaves.

Then we pile them up
with our rakes
and have a bonfire.

A tree is nice because
it has a trunk and limbs.
     We can climb the tree
and see over all the yards.
     We can sit on a limb
and think about things.

Or play pirate ship
up in the tree.
    If it is an apple tree
we can climb it
to pick the apples.

Cats get away from dogs
by going up the tree.

Birds build nests in trees
and live there.

Sticks come
off the trees too.

We draw in the sand
with the sticks.

A tree is nice
to hang a swing in.
Or a basket of flowers.
It is a good place to lean
your hoe while you rest.

A tree is nice
because it makes shade.
The cows lie down
in the shade when it is hot.

People have picnics
there too.
And the baby takes his nap
in his buggy in the shade.

A tree is nice
for a house to be near.

The tree shades the house
and keeps it cool.

The tree holds off the wind
and keeps the wind from blowing
the roof off the house sometimes.

A tree is nice to plant.

You dig the biggest hole
you can and put the little
tree in.

Then you pour in lots
of water and then the dirt.

You hang the shovel
back in the garage.

Every day for years and YEARS
you watch the little tree grow.

You say to people,
"I planted that tree."

They wish they had one
so they go home
and plant a tree too.

Sharing Time

1. How do the children have fun
   with the trees?

2. How does a tree help
   people and animals?

3. How would you plant a tree?

4. Why do you think a tree
   is nice?

Clouds

Dorothy Aldis

If I had a spoon
As tall as the sky
I'd dish out the clouds
That go slip-sliding by.

I'd take them right in
And give them to cook
And see if they tasted
As good as they look.

Spring Rain

Marchette Chute

The storm came up so very quick
　　It couldn't have been quicker.
I should have brought my hat along,
　　I should have brought my slicker.

My hair is wet, my feet are wet,
　　I couldn't be much wetter.
I fell into a river once
　　But this is even better.

One Was Johnny

Maurice Sendak

1 was Johnny who
lived by himself

2 was a rat who
jumped on his shelf

3 was a cat who

chased the rat

4 was a dog who

came in and sat

5 was a turtle who
bit the dog's tail

6 was a monkey who
brought in the mail

7 a blackbird pecked
poor Johnny's nose

8 was a tiger out
selling old clothes

9 was a robber who
took an old shoe

10 was a puzzle.
What should Johnny do?

He stood
on a chair
and said,
"Here's what I'll do—
I'll start
to count backwards
and when
I am through—
if this house
isn't empty
I'll eat
all of you!!!!"

9 was the robber who
left looking pale

8 was the tiger who
chased him to jail

7 the blackbird flew
off to Havana

6 was the monkey who
stole a banana

5 was the turtle who
crawled off to bed

4 was the dog who
slid home on a sled

3 was the cat who
pounced on the rat

2 was the rat who

left with the cat

1 was Johnny who

lived by himself

AND LIKED IT LIKE THAT!

Sharing Time

1. Who came to Johnny's house?

2. What was the funniest thing
   that happened?

3. How did Johnny feel
   when his house was full?

4. How was Johnny clever?

5. If all the animals came
   to *your* house, what
   would you do?

Star Light, Star Bright

Star light, star bright,
The first star I see tonight,
I wish I may, I wish I might
Have the wish I wish tonight.